FAULTY FOUNDATIONS

Pastor Seyi Ogunorunyinka

PREFACE

What is your life built upon? Is it built upon a lasting foundation that will sustain you through the storms of life or is it built on a faulty foundation that will fail at the first sign of shaking?

Just as the foundation of a building determines if that building will stand or fall, the foundation of your life will determine if you will be successful or if you will end up as a failure. Remember that the race for salvation is one of endurance and it is only those who are still standing at the end who will win the prize. You may be standing strong today but do you know what tomorrow holds?

As Christians, we should only build on one foundation: our Lord Jesus Christ. He is the firm foundation that will enable us to go through this life as winners and make it to our eternal rest in heaven. If you profess to be a child of God, are you sure that your life is built upon the solid rock that is Jesus Christ?

This book explains the importance of foundations in our lives and examines the reasons why so many Christians today are finding it difficult to live the lives that God has called them to. It explains what we as children of God have to do to emerge victorious at the end of the race.

I pray that as you read this book you will receive a fresh revelation from the Lord that will strengthen your faith and improve your relationship with him.

CONTENTS

CHAPTER 1

IMPORTANCE OF FOUNDATIONS

Psalm 11:3 states, **"If the foundations are faulty what can the righteous do?"**

Do you know what kind of foundation your life is built upon? Your foundation plays a very important role in determining if your life will be a success or a failure. The ultimate goal of a meaningful life is to end up in heaven but with the wrong foundation, this will be an impossible task.

The dictionary defines a foundation as the basis on which a thing stands, Is founded, or is supported. To illustrate the importance of a foundation, we will examine the role that foundations play in buildings.

If you look around any major city in the world today, you will see a wide variety of buildings: big ones and small ones, one storey buildings and multi-storey skyscrapers. Some buildings are more aesthetically pleasing while others are more functional, some are very expensive while others are more basic. Each building was created to fulfil a certain purpose whether it is to serve as a home for a family to live in, a church where the Lord is worshipped, an office where business is transacted or a school where children are educated. Despite the diversity in the form and function of buildings, however, they all have one thing in common: a foundation.

A building's foundation is the platform upon which it is erected. It is usually made from concrete and it serves to transfer the weight of the building to the ground below. It has to be specifically designed to enable it to carry the weight of the building which is being constructed.

While a foundation does not add anything to the beauty of a building, without a suitable foundation, a building, no matter how beautiful it may be, will be unstable and will therefore not be fit for purpose. A building's foundation can therefore be said to be the most important yet the least visible part of the structure.

When you want to lay a foundation, the first thing you need to know is the type of building that you want to construct. The foundation that you need for a bungalow is different from the foundation that you need if you want to build a multi-storey skyscraper. There are a wide variety of foundations and the type that you design will determine how high or how heavy the structure you can build is.

You do not have to be an expert at construction or an architect or engineer to recognize how important it is to have a strong, solid foundation for any structure. Every now and then, we read stories in the newspapers of buildings that have collapsed, injuring and killing many. The primary reason for most of these collapses is the fact that the foundation was not strong enough to withstand the weight of the building.

In the same way that the foundation of a building determines how heavy or high it can be, the foundation of your life determines how much God can bless you.

We are all building our lives just as a contractor builds a building. Every day, we add one or more bricks to the structure that will only be fully complete when we have breathed our last breath. The foundations of our lives are our beliefs, the things we hold to be true. They are the primary determinants of all that we do; our thoughts, our words and our actions.

If your foundation is not right, if it is not solid enough, then God cannot bless you to the extent that he would want to. Philippians 4:19 states, **"And my God shall supply all your need according to his riches in glory by Christ Jesus."**

All God's promises in the bible apply to you. Acts 10:34 states, **"then Peter opened his mouth and said": "in truth, I perceive that God shows no partiality."** God is not a respecter of persons. He desires to bless you as much as he does anyone else. If you feel that your life is not where it should be and that despite how hard you work you are not being blessed as much as you expect, you need to take a long, hard look at yourself and at your foundation.

Can your foundation carry the blessing, increase and prosperity that God wants to place on you? God is not going to waste his investments on you if he knows that your life will not be able to carry blessings.

I am sure that many other servants of God have experienced the frustration that I sometimes feel when the sermons that I preach seem to fall on deaf ears. In my year of ministry, I have said the same things over and over again to certain people but I have yet to see any visible change in their attitude and actions. It is difficult to understand why a man who professes to desire real change in his life is reluctant to listen to the word of God and to consistently adhere to that word. I have come to realise that the problem is one of a faulty foundation. If a foundation is faulty, no matter how much righteous seed you sow into that life nothing will grow on it.

In the parable of the sower in **Mark 4**, Jesus described a particular type of person in **Verse 15** as follows: "**And these are the ones by the wayside where the word is sown. When they hear, Satan comes immediately and takes away the word that was sown in their hearts**".

The type of person that Jesus is referring to here is someone whose heart is too hardened for the word to make any real impression on. Such people hear the word of God and see the effects that same word is having on the lives of those around them who decide to abide by it. They are surrounded by the awesomeness of God but they find it difficult to change because of their faulty foundations.

Other people hear the word and strive to abide by it but they are not able to. They recognize that holiness is an essential requirement for heaven and they try very hard to be holy but their polluted foundation makes it impossible for them to do so.

If a foundation is faulty, no matter how holy or righteous the person may try to be, he will never succeed because his foundation is not capable of supporting that holiness. On the other hand, the things that people with faulty foundations find difficult to achieve are very easy for those who have solid foundations.

In the same way that the foundation is the platform upon which a building is built, so is your foundation the platform upon which your life is built. What will eventually happen to a structure, whether it will stand or fall, is dependent on the types of foundation that it has and what happens to a destiny, whether it will be successful or not, depends on the type of foundation that is supporting it.

If you happen to be in an exalted position in life, the determinant of how long you will stay in that position and how long your blessings will last will depend on your foundation. If a foundation can only support a one storey building and you put two storey's on it, sooner or later cracks will begin to appear around the building, the more floors you add to the building the more cracks you will see and before you know it, the whole building will eventually crumble.

In the same way, some lives cannot sustain too many blessings before they start to fall apart. This is the reason why so many people sort off very well in life but eventually lose everything.

The way you start something goes a long way to determining how that thing will end and so your foundation is the very first step to many steps in your life.

Your foundation is what brought you from where you started to where you are now and it is what will take you to where you will be tomorrow. It is easy to blame other factors for the state of our lives today. Household wickedness, household witchcraft, unfriendly friends and many more usually take the blame for the fact that our lives are not where we expect them to be. The truth of the matter though is that our actions, as a result of our faulty foundations, have made us what we are today.

Your foundation will determine the heights you can reach and whether or not you will be able to withstand the storms of life.

In earthquake-prone areas of the world, the types of foundations that are normally used to construct buildings are a special fortified type.   This type of foundation enables the buildings to bear up against the shaking of the earth that occurs during earthquakes and still remain standing.

Is your foundation strong enough to withstand the wickedness of this world? Can it help you survive the affliction that you may face, the illnesses and inexplicable infirmity that may come your way, the evil culture that surrounds you and the wind of stagnancy that may periodically blow over your life?

Some people do not have foundations that can withstand any storms. The moment they experience any attack on their lives, they want to die. If they happened to suffer financial loss, they immediately feel like committing suicide. Faced with the slightest difficulty, they are ready to give up. If you do not have a solid foundation, you will be the number one candidate for the wickedness of this world.

A child who was not exposed to trials and challenges and whose parents always shielded him from the reality of life will have a very different outlook from a child who had to grow up on the streets.

Someone, who growing up never felt hunger was always driven everywhere by drivers in air-conditioned cars with an accompanying nanny, who never experienced any problems and is totally ignorant of the real world will find it very difficult if he is suddenly left to fend for himself. If such a child should lose his parents and have to face the storms of life, those storms will likely destroy the child. This is because his parents failed to lay the type of foundation for him that would carry him through life.

It is for this reason that when I was growing up, my parents always wanted me to experience what he called, "the other side of life." They wanted me to know what life was really about so that if I had to fend for myself, I would not be too ignorant of reality. They were trying to lay down a suitable foundation for my life.

Your foundation is the number one determinant of whether you will succeed in life or not. If your foundation is faulty and nothing is done to put it right, then lasting success and the reward of eternal life will be difficult for you to achieve. The kind of weight that a building can take is dependent on the type of foundation that it has. In the same way, the outcome of your destiny will depend on the type of foundation supporting it.

CHAPTER 2
DO YOU HAVE A FAULTY FOUNDATION?

Having examined what a foundation is and noted its importance to our destiny we will now consider the cause of faulty foundations. When I refer to faulty foundations here, I am not talking about the impact that the actions of our more recent forefathers have on our lives.

Many Africans suffer from this type of negative inheritance, as their ancestors engaged in many evil and occultist practises that are still capable of affecting their lives today. The foundations that I am talking about go back much further to our very first ancestors, they go back to the beginning, to the time of the creation of the earth.

We can find the story of the creation of the earth in Genesis 1. This is a chapter of the bible that we all know very well. Before God created man, he first created the heavens and the earth. He made light and divided the light from the darkness that was there before; He made the earth and separated the water from the land; he created all the plants and the animals. He did all these things in distinct phases and he made sure that everything was perfect with one phase before he moved on to the next.

The sentence "and God saw that it was; good" is repeated often in Genesis 1 to reflect God's satisfaction with all that he had created. By the time God had finished with his creation, everything on earth was perfect and ready and God had laid a solid foundation for his final creation: Adam.

Adam and Eve were created with a solid foundation. Everything about them, their lives and their situation was faultless. Genesis 1:27 tells us that they were created in God's image and so they were perfect. They also had freedom of choice; they could choose what they wanted to do. Adam and Eve were capable of reaching any height that they aspired to as long as they operated within the confines of the rules that God had set for them.

The most important rule that God gave Adam can be found in Genesis 2:16 which states, "**And the Lord God commanded the man, saying "of every tree of the garden you may freely eat; but of the tree of the knowledge of good and evil you shall not eat, for in the day that you eat of it you shall surely die**".

The bible tells us in Genesis 3 however, that the serpent deceived Eve into eating the forbidden fruit and that she gave some of it to Adam who also ate. Adam and Eve had the free will to choose whether or not to obey God and as a result of their choice to disobey, they were cast out of the garden of Eden

The consequence of Adam and Eve's disobedience to God was spiritual separation from God and physical death.

Sin came into the world and has been here ever since. Romans 5:12-14 states, "**Therefore just as through one man sin entered the world, and death through sin, and thus death spread to all men, because all sinned, for until the law sin was in the world, but sin is not imputed when there is no law. Nevertheless, death reigned from Adam to Moses, even over those who had not sinned according to the likeness of the transgression of Adam, who is a type of him who was to come**".

This bible verse clearly explains the concept of original sin. Through Adam, sin became an intrinsic part of the human race. Every descendant of Adam comes into the world with the sinful nature embedded into his constitution, even if he has not yet sinned in the way that Adam did. As the father of the human race, Adam had a negative impact on his descendants and we all share this definitive negative inheritance: Sin.

Our inheritance from Adam is our sinful corrupt nature.

The bible says in Romans 3:23. "**For all have sinned and fall short of the glory of God.**" There is no exception to this; everyone born of man shares the propensity to corruption and sin

How can we define sin?

When we think of sin, we tend to think about breaking the ten commandments that God gave Moses. Sin however is much more than just the breaking of the commandments or the disregard of God's law, it is the very nature of the human heart, which thinks, speaks and acts evil and neglects all good, which demands its will and is opposed to God's will

After Adam and Eve were banished from the garden of Eden, sin quickly spread amongst humanity in Genesis 4, we can find details of the first death in the world, which occurred through murder when Cain murdered his brother Abel out of envy, jealousy and bitterness. Things gradually got worse until depravity filled the earth. We can see the extent to which sin had penetrated humanity in Genesis 6:5 which states, **"Then the Lord saw that the wickedness of man was great in the earth and that every intent of the thoughts of his heart was only evil continually."**

In a few short generations, man had moved from being perfect, as he was when God created him, to be filled with wickedness. This bible verse tells us that God looked at man and saw that his heart had become desperately wicked and that he was doing evil intentionally. Man's corrupt heart was the source of all the iniquity in the world. The heart of man is ruled by his selfish desires with no regard for God or anyone else. Is it any wonder then that at this time the earth was filled with violence, depravity and lawlessness?

With every man focused on satisfying the evil lusts of his heart, the world must have been a place of destruction and despair. Through their investigation of fossils dating back to the time of the flood, anthropologists have discovered that cannot cannibalism and violence were rife in the world at this time

Due to the sin that came into the world through Adam, people are selfish by nature.

Unfortunately, loving God wholeheartedly and following His Word as He desires us to do does not come naturally or easily to us. Rather, we are wired by our sinful nature to seek to serve our interests at all times and to reject the Word of God. Even when we try to do the right thing, we generally do it to feel better about ourselves which is the wrong motive.

The outcome of the fall of man is numerous and deadly. The first major consequence is spiritual blindness. 2 Corinthians 4:4 speaks of those, "**whose minds the god of this age had blinded, who do not believe.**" The glory of God is everywhere; His awesome love toward us, his holiness, mercy and forgiveness, are clear to those who have spiritual sight.

However, those whose eyes Satan has closed are blind to it.

The next consequence of man's fall is his self-centeredness and self-reliance. Man is filled with useless pride and selfish ambition and because he has been blinded by Satan, he puts his trust in earthly possessions, forgetting that life is uncertain and that its length depends wholly on the almighty God.

We can see an example of this in James 4:13-14, "**come now, you who say, "Today or tomorrow we will go to such and such a city, spend a year there, buy and sell, and make a profit"; whereas you do not know what will happen tomorrow. For what is our life? It is even a vapour that appears for a little time and then vanishes away.**" Satan blinds man to his mortality and makes him focus instead on useless pursuits which will in the long run lead to his eternal damnation.

The lust of the flesh is another product of sin. Galatians 5:19-21 states, "**now the works of the flesh are evident, which are: adultery, fornication, uncleanness, lewdness, idolatry, sorcery, hatred, contentions, jealousies, outbursts of wrath, selfish ambitions, dissensions, heresies, envy, murders, drunkenness, revelries, and the like.**" These are the products of man's corrupt nature and they come naturally to fallen man. No one has to teach man to commit these sinful acts; they come naturally to him.

Worldliness is also another outcome of man's fall. I John 2:16 defines it as, "**the lust of the flesh, the lust of the eyes, and the pride of life.**"

Many believe that worldliness is limited to our external actions but it is internal because it begins in the corrupt heart of man.

As the bible verse states, worldliness is characterised by three attitudes; the lust of the flesh which is the fixation on satisfying man's physical desires, the lust of the eyes which is longing for and amassing materials goods and the pride of life which is an obsession with making a name for oneself or gaining position and status. Preoccupation and focus on the things of the world make it impossible to focus on God and do his will.

Man is weak and is powerless to free himself from Satan's grip. Romans 8:21 states that the human race is held in the "bondage of corruption". The New American Standard Version of the Bible translates this phrase as "slavery to corruption." When you are enslaved to something, it means you cannot free yourself from that thing no matter how hard you try. Jeremiah 13:23 states, "**can the Ethiopian change his skin or the leopard its spots? Then may you also do good who are accustomed to do evil.**"

This is why Apostle Paul says in Romans 7: 15-24, "**for what I am doing, I do not understand. For what I will to do, that I do not practice; but what I hate, that I do. If, then, I do what I will not to do, I agree with the law that it is good. But now, it is no longer I who do it, but sin that dwells in me. For I know that in me (that is, in my flesh) nothing good dwells; for to will is present with me, but how to perform what is good I do not find. For the good that I will to do, I do not do; but the evil I will not to do, that I practice. Now if I do what I will not to do, it is no longer I who do it, but sin that dwells in me. I find then a law, that evil is present with me, the one who wills to do good. For I delight in the law of God according to the inward man. But I see another law in my members, warning against the law of my mind, and bringing me into captivity to the law of sin which is in my members. O wretched man that I am! Who will deliver me from this body of death?**"

The bible states, in Romans 3:10, "**there is none righteous, no, not one.**"

Therefore, the issue of sin applies to every single person born of man. The only human beings that can be said to be free of the burden of the inheritance of sin are Adam and Eve who were created in God's image and were perfect and our Lord Jesus Christ, who is a special case because he was conceived by the holy spirit through the virgin Mary.

Even David, who was referred to as a man after God's heart in 1 Samuel 13:14 could not boast of a solid foundation and he attested to this in Psalms 51. We are told in Psalms 51:1 that David wrote the psalm when "**Nathan the prophet went to him, after he had gone into Bathsheba**". Verse 5 states, "**Behold, I was brought forth in iniquity, and in sin, my mother conceived me.**" David was not saying that he was conceived in sin and born out of wedlock. What he was referring to here is the natural inclination to evil that we all bring into this world with us and which is the root of all our wrongdoing. He was acknowledging that his true nature was fallen and that the innermost desires and purposes of his heart were evil.

We have now established that as a result of our common ancestor Adam's transgressions, we all share a sinful nature. No matter how hard we may try to walk in righteousness and obey the word of god, it is not in our nature to do so. Sooner or later, our sinful nature will take control of our actions and we will do something that goes against the word of God.

Man's sinful nature is the root cause of his faulty foundations. The foundations of all our lives have been compromised from the beginning as a result of our negative inheritance from Adam. No matter how hard we may try to build on these faulty foundations, sooner or later, the cracks in our lives will begin to show and eventually, everything will come crumbling down. Some of us may be more successful than others at shoring up the structures of our lives, but sooner or later, anything that was built on the faulty foundations of our human nature will fail.

CHAPTER 3

THE NATION OF ISRAEL AND THE MAKING OF A KING

To illustrate the effects that faulty foundations can have on our destinations, we are going to examine the nation of Israel and the making of king Saul, who as Israel's first king holds a very special place in history. An examination of the events which led up to Saul being appointed king, his reign and the way he ultimately lost his kingdom will be very illuminating in our examination of faulty foundations.

As I stated in chapter two, after the fall of man, the world quickly become filled with violence and iniquity. Man under the direction of Satan was consumed by wickedness and evil. Angered at what man had become, God sent the flood to wipe out all humanity, except Noah, and his sons. He then established a convent with Abraham. One of the descendants of Noah's son, Shem.

Genesis 17:7 states, "**And I will establish my covenant between me and you and your descendants after you in their generations, for an everlasting covenant, to be God to you and your descendant after you**".

The children of Israel were Abraham's descendants and following his covenant with their ancestors, God blessed Israel and set them apart from all the other nations. He rescued them from bondage in Egypt and established them to be his special people.

Deuteronomy 7:6 states, "**for you are a holy people to the Lord your God; the Lord your God has chosen you to be a people for Himself, a special treasure above all the people on the face of the earth**".

God set apart the nation of Israel and blessed them so that they would be witnesses for him in the world. He wanted other nations to look at the children of Israel, and see that they were different because Jehovah, the one true God was on their side. They had a special relationship with him that no other nations had and Moses reminded them of this in Deuteronomy 4:32-34 which states, **"for ask now concerning the days that are past, which were before you since the day that God created man on the earth, and ask from one end of heaven to the other, whether any great thing like this has happened, or anything like has been heard. Did any people ever hear the voice of God speaking out of the midst of the fire, as you have heard, and live? Or did God ever try to go and take for himself a nation from the midst of another nation, by trials, by signs, by wonders, by war, by a mighty and an outstretched arm and by great errors according to all that he Lord your God did for you in Egypt before your eyes?"**

God gave that nation of Israel detailed instructions as to how He wanted them to live. He made it clear that if they followed his commandments, then he would bless them abundantly. The idea was that all the other nations around would see how much Israel was being blessed and would also begin to worship God. If, however, the children of Israel forgot the Lord and his commandments and began to live like the other nations around them, then the Lord would forsake them.

Unfortunately, the children of Israel failed to keep up their end of the bargain because their faulty foundations negatively impacted their ability to obey God and follow his commandments. However, God was merciful to them and sent judges to guide them in their times of trouble.

During this period judges, such as Deborah, Samson and Gideon were appointed by God at particular times and for specific reasons, to lead the nation of Israel. This remained the normal course of things until the children of Israel demanded a king to be set over them.

The build-up to Saul's becoming the first king of Israel can be found in 1 Samuel 8. Up until this point, the nation of Israel was a theocracy, which means that it had a government that was ruled by religious authority. God ruled through judges and also through his prophets. At the time that Saul became king, Israel was being governed by Samuel.

1 Samuel 8:1-5 states, "**now it came to pass when Samuel was old that he made his sons judges over Israel. The name of his firstborn was Joel, and the name of his second, Abijah; they were judges in Beersheba. But his sons did not walk in his ways; they turned aside after dishonest gain, took bribes, and prevented justice. Then all the elders of Israel gathered together and came to Samuel at Ramah, and said to him, "look, you are old, and your sons do not walk in your ways. Now make us a king to judge us like all the nations**".

Before this, Israel had no other king but God. He was the ultimate authority and the one to whom all the previous judges and prophets turned when a decision was to be made or direction was required. At this time, however, the children of Israel were dissatisfied with the existing arrangement. Samuel was old and could no longer govern as he had before, so he appointed his sons as judges over Israel. Unfortunately, Samuels sons were wicked men who like many of the children of Israel did not fear God and who used their positions for their gain.

The children of Israel's response to this was to request that Samuel appoint a king to rule over them. They specifically asked for a king "to judge us like all the nation." (verse 5).

It is interesting to note that they did not ask for another judge to be appointed to replace Samuel's sons, rather they asked for an entirely new system of governance. The reason for this was that they were unhappy with the current system and wanted to be like all the other nations around them who had kings ruling over them.

The children of Israel failed to recognize the privileged position that they were in. Why would they wish to be like other nations when God had separated them unto himself to be special? Why would they want to emulate the other nations that they had been called to be a witness to?

God brought them out of their bondage in Egypt so that they would be a special people to him on the earth distinct from all the others who were doing evil in his sight. Unfortunately, because of their faulty foundations, they did not appreciate or understand God's purpose for their lives; their foundations prevented them from walking in his word and doing his will.

Time and time again they would turn away from him and follow the dictates of their hearts and time and time again they would suffer terribly as a result. Each time they were afflicted, they would suddenly remember their God and run back to him. However, as soon as he delivered them from their enemies, their backsliding would commence once again. No wonder God called them "stiff-necked" people.

In asking Samuel to appoint a king over them, the children of Israel were once again exhibiting their willfulness and their lack of understanding. They did not realize that in asking for a human king, they were effectively rejecting God as their king. When they were faced with the problems of Samuel's wayward sons, rather than turning to God and seeking his will, they began to look at the other nations around them.

On numerous occasions, the Lord had told the children of Israel not to imitate the actions of the other nations around them.

In Leviticus 20:23, He said, "**And you shall not walk in the statutes of the nation which I am casting out before you.**"

These other nations were supposed to imitate the nation of Israel and not the other way around. In their obstinacy, however, the children of Israel decided that what they needed most then was to be like everyone else around them.

Another reason that the children of Israel gave Samuel for wanting a king appointed over them was so that "our King may judge us and go out before us and fight our battles." (1 Samuel 8:20) Looking around at the other nations, the children of Israel may have felt inadequate because they did not have a splendidly attired monarch to give the direction and to fight their battles for them. Their eyes were blinded to the fact that there is none better to have on your side, no warrior mightier than the Most High God who is mighty in battle.

In response to the request for a king to be appointed over them god told Samuel in 1 Samuel 8:7-9, "**heed the voice of the people in** all that they say to you; for they had not rejected you, but they have rejected me, that I should not reign over them. According to all the works which they have done since the day that I brought them up out of Egypt, even to this day with which they have forsaken me and served other gods so they are doing to you also. Now, therefore, heed their voice. However, you shall solemnly forewarn them, and show them the behaviour of the king who will reign over them."

Samuel duly informed the children of Israel all that the Lord had told him concerning the problems that the appointment of asking would bring to the nation but they still insisted that their will and not the Lord's will be done and that a king be appointed.

Despite everything that the Lord had done for the children of Israel, they were still not able to put aside their own will and accede to his will. Their faulty foundations, inherited from Adam, were once again instrumental in their deviation from the plans that the Lord had for them.

At this juncture, God did provide a king for the nation of Israel but as is stated in psalm 106:15, "**he gave them their request, but sent leanness into their soul.**" As the introduction of the monarchy into the nation of Israel was built upon this faulty foundation, upon the will of man and not the will of God, the children of Israel would ultimately have to pay the price for their failure to follow the dictates of the Almighty.

The man that God chose to be king of Israel was Saul. Outwardly, Saul fit the part of a king. The bible tells us in 1 Samuel 9:2 that he was "choice and handsome". It further states, "There was not a more handsome person than he among the children of Israel. From his shoulder upward he was taller than any of the people." It seemed that God was determined that the new king should as much as possible fit the image of a king that the children of Israel had in their heads.

Saul was the son of Kish, who is described in 1 Samuel 9:1 as "a mighty man of power."

This means that he was a man of wealth and substance and as such, Saul came from a privileged background despite this background, however, he was still only a member of the tribe of

Benjamin which was the smallest of the tribes of Israel and amongst the Benjamites, Saul's family was also the smallest. For this reason, Saul was surprised when Samuel informed him that he would become king of Israel.

I Samuel 9:21 states, "**And Saul answered and said, "Am I not a Benjamite, of the smallest of the tribes of Israel, and my family the least of all the families of the tribes of Benjamin? Why then do you speak like this to me?**"

At this stage, Saul was very humble and modest. He was not self-seeking nor did he count himself to be worthy of the honour that was to be bestowed on him. He must have been even more astonished when Samuel invited him to dine with him that evening.

1 Samuel 9:22 states that Samuel gave Saul "The place of honour", at the dinner, which must have been attended by the area's most influential people, as these were the type of people who Samuel would have ordinarily dined with. As if that was not enough, Samuel also gave Saul the choicest portion of the meat that was being served. It must have been evident to all who witnessed this dinner that something very special was happening. Why would Samuel, the most important man in all the nation of Israel pay such attention and give such honour to a man like Saul if not that God had ordered him to?

It is important to note the kind of relationship that Samuel and Saul had at first. At the time in question, Samuel was the most powerful man in the nation of Israel. In addition to being the judge, he was also the first prophet of the Lord in the nation.

A prophet can be defined as a spokesperson for God, someone who enjoins, forewarns, instructs inspires, intercedes, teaches and counsels the people of God. He brings the word of God to the people of God and urges them to do his will. Samuel had delivered the children of Israel from the philistines through the power of prayer and it was he who, upon direction from the Lord, instructed the Israelites to put away all their false gods and turn back to the Lord. Given all of this, Saul must have stood in awe of Samuel.

It is clear from reading the first half of 1 Samuel 10 that Saul listened very carefully to everything that Samuel told him and carried out his instructions fully. He was like a baby who did not know his right from left and he allowed himself to be directed and counselled by Samuel.

In 1 Samuel 10:1-7, Samuel gave Saul several signs to look out for which would show that indeed he was speaking the truth and the Lord had chosen Saul to be king.

The final sign is found in 1 Samuel 10:6 "**then the spirit of the Lord will come upon you, and you will prophesy with them and be turned into another man.**"

Everything that Samuel told Saul would happen came to pass and Saul was transformed into a new man and prophesied with the prophets that he met on his way home. Despite this confirmation that he had been chosen to be king, the spirit of humility was still upon Saul. This was no more evident than in 1 Samuel 10 when the lots were drawn to choose a king and his name was picked. Instead of appearing before the people, Saul, feeling unworthy of the position to which he had been named, hid amongst the baggage.

Despite his initial misgivings, Saul was eventually named the first king of Israel. We shall examine the effect that this stratospheric elevation had on his character and determine whether his foundations were strong enough to carry his new position in the next chapter.

CHAPTER 4

SAUL THE KING

In the previous chapter, we looked at how the children of Israel, due to their faulty foundation, turned away from the plans that God had for their nation and demanded that a king be set over them.

God chose Saul, a man who had all the outward qualities of a king, to rule them. He was tall, handsome and had an imposing regal presence, one that was befitting a king. God chose Saul; He carried out a transformation on his inner man.

1 Samuel 10:9 says of Saul, **"so it was when he had turned his back to go from Samuel, that God gave him another heart; and all those signs came to pass that day."**

The bible does not tell us much about Saul's personality before he became king. Apart from his height and his good looks, he does not seem to have much to distinguish him from the next man. He certainly appeared to be modest and humble, as evidenced by his initial reaction to the news that he was to become king but his later actions seem to prove that underneath the appearance of goodness, something more evil was lurking, waiting to emerge.

Even though Saul did not have a character that was suitable for a king after Samuel had anointed him, the Lord changed his heart and gave him another one. This new heart so transformed him that those who had known him before were astounded by his new qualities.

In 1 Samuel 10:11 upon witnessing Saul prophesying with a band of prophets one such person was moved to comment "is

Saul also among the prophets?"

It is important to remember Saul's background. Even though he came from a well to do family, his primary concern must have been with the care of his father's agricultural holdings as evidenced by his long search for the missing donkeys and the fact that after he had been named as king he returned to his farming duties. He does not seem to have had any relevant experience, either as a warrior or as a prophet of God to recommend him for the role. Everything that he was able to achieve after being named king was a result of the power of God which was working within him. Saul in himself was unsuitable to be king.

After Saul was named as the new king of Israel, he returned to his duties on his father's farm. It was while carrying out these duties that he heard about the threat of the ammonites. 1 Samuel 11:6 states, "**then the spirit of God came upon Saul when he heard this news, and his anger was greatly aroused.**"

The spirit of God roused Saul's fury and inspired him with all the qualities he needed including strength, wisdom and courage, to put together an army and lead them to victory against the ammonites. It was after this victory that Saul was officially crowned king of Israel.

It appears that the first two years of Saul's reign were good ones. Settling into his new position as king, he must have continued to rely on Samuel and by extension on God for guidance. An example of this is when he showed wisdom by not acceding to the death of those who had initially opposed his rules and gave God the glory for his victories. This we find in 1 Samuel 11:13 which states, "**But Saul said, "Not a man shall be put to death this day, for today the Lord has accomplished salvation in Israel**".

However, this show of wisdom and humility was all soon to change. The power of being a king and a victorious commander went to Saul's head and his true character was eventually revealed. The true nature of a man's character is usually exposed when he gains power and wealth.

For themselves, power and wealth do not change a man. They merely reveal what was hidden Saul's major flaw was a lack of trust in God and an overblown sense of his worth. If you have a faulty foundation will be difficult for you to remain grounded and to trust in God when you are elevated to lofty heights.

The first sign that Saul was changing from the humble and wise man who knew that he was only an emissary of the true king of Israel Jehovah, to the willful monarch that he would become can be found in 1 Samuel 13.

In this chapter, the nation of Israel was facing attack from a mighty Philistine army and the number of soldiers with Saul was inadequate to defeat them. The only way that the children of Israel would prevail was if the Lord himself were to step into the situation.

Before a battle, it was customary for the children of Israel to make a sacrifice to the Lord so that he would assist them in the battle and the task of giving the offering fell to the priest. Samuel had given Saul instructions to wait for him for seven days and he would come and tell him what to do and offer the sacrifice to God. However, when the seventh day dawned and Samuel still had not arrived, Saul decided to offer the sacrifice to the Lord himself.

In offering the sacrifice to the Lord himself, Saul showed that he believed he no longer needed Samuel and that he could do everything on his own. He acted as though the fact that he was king put him on equal or even higher standing with the prophet and permitted him to do whatever he wanted, regardless of the directives that he had previously been given

1 Samuel 13:10-12 states, "**Now it happened, as soon as he had finished presenting the burnt offering, that Samuel came; and Saul went out to meet him, that he might greet him. And Samuel said, "What have you done?" And Saul said, "When I saw that the people were scattered from me, and that you did not come within the days appointed, and that the Philistines gathered together at Michmash, then I said, 'The Philistines will now come down on me at Gilgal, and I have not made supplication to the Lord.' Therefore I felt compelled, and offered a burnt offering.**"

Rather than being repentant, Saul seems strangely pleased that he was able to carry out the offering himself and it appears that he had no idea of the wrong that he had done. He reasoned that Samuel was to be blamed for not arriving within the time frame that he had given and could therefore not have expected him to continue to wait while the threat of the philistines was hanging over all their heads, he continued to justify his disobedience, citing the fact that all his people were leaving out of fear and that he had to force himself to give the offering because he could not go to battle without calling on the Lord.

Samuel did not buy any of the excuses that Saul gave and stated in 1 Samuel 13:13-14, "**You have done foolishly. You have not kept the commandment of the Lord your God, which he commanded you, for now, the Lord would have established your kingdom over Israel forever. But now your kingdom shall not continue. The Lord has sought for Himself a man after his own heart, and the Lord has commanded him to be commander over his people because you have not kept what the Lord commanded you.**"

Saul's actions here were more than foolish. They showed a blatant disregard for the sacrifice, the priesthood, and God's command, he selfishly acted of his own accord and in disobedience to God. In his own eyes, he may have thought that he was doing the right thing by offering the sacrifice but God does not care what seems right to us. All he cares about is that we obey Him.

The willfulness and impetuousness of Saul's character continued to be exposed in various forms throughout his reign and revealed that he was not a man who could be trusted with power and authority. One key incident which is highlighted in 1 Samuel 14 was the rash curse of death that he placed on anyone who broke the fast he had imposed on his soldiers and his determination to kill his son Jonathan who had unknowingly broken the fast.

The final straw which cost Saul his kingdom was his flagrant disobedience to God's command concerning the Amalekites in 1 Samuel 15. We can already see the deterioration of the previously close relationship between Samuel and Saul in the way that Samuel relayed Gods message to Saul.

1 Samuel 15:1 states, "**Samuel also said to Saul, "the LORD sent me to anoint you king over his people, over Israel. Now, therefore, heed the voice of the words of the LORD**"

With these words, Samuel was reminding Saul exactly who he was and the relationship that they used to have before Saul got carried away by his position. He was also pointing out to Saul that the position that he held was given to him by the Lord and that it was therefore in Saul's best interest to obey his commands. We can only imagine the behaviour that Saul must have exhibited for Samuel to have been compelled to speak to him in such a manner and to remain him of facts that he should not have had to be reminded about.

The Lord's orders to Saul were quite straightforward.

1 Samuel 15:13 states, "**Now go and attack Amalek, and utterly destroy all that they have, and do not spare them. But kill both man and woman, infant and nursing child, ox and sheep, camel and donkey.**"

It was customary for soldiers to take plunder and slaves from a battle as their pay but the Lord's instructions of total annihilation of the Amalekites were very clear in this case. This was an opportunity for Saul to redeem himself after the debacle in Gilgal when he overstepped his bounds and offered a sacrifice to the Lord instead of waiting for Samuel to do it.

With the help of the Lord, the battle against the Amalekites was successful but instead of doing as he had been instructed, Saul decided to improve upon the Lord's instructions. 1 Samuel 15:9 states, "**But Saul and the people spared Agag and the best of the sheep, the oxen, the fatlings, the lambs, and all that was good, and are unwilling to utterly destroy them. But everything despised and worthless, that they utterly destroyed.**"

Saul only followed the Lord's commandments for as long as it was convenient for him to do so; it was easy enough to destroy the worthless items but he disobeyed and kept all the valuable livestock for himself and his men and also spared the life of Agag the king of the Amalekites.

After the battle was over, Saul then went to Carmel to set up a monument to himself before proceeding to Gilgal. The setting up of the monument to glorify himself shows the depth to which Saul had sunk. It is a far cry from the Saul that we saw at the beginning of his reign who was quick to give God the glory for his victories.

When Samuel eventually caught up with him, Saul was quick to greet him and assure him that he had carried out all the Lord's instructions. 1 Samuel 15:13-15 states, "**Then Samuel went to Saul, and Saul said to him, "Blessed are you of the LORD! I have performed the commandment of the Lord." But Samuel said, "what then is this bleating of the sheep in my ears, and the lowing of the oxen which I hear?" And Saul said, "They have brought them from the Amalekites; for the people spared the best of the sheep and the oxen, to sacrifice to the Lord your God; and the rest we have utterly destroyed.**"

Saul's response to Samuel is typical of the egotistic despot that he had become. He refused to accept any blame for his failure to carry out the Lord's instructions, choosing instead to lay it at the feet of his men. His excuse that he had allowed some of the animals to be spared so that they could be offered to the Lord as a sacrifice was merely an attempt to hide his disobedience and selfishness under the guise of holiness.

Samuel's response to Saul's excuses was firm and unequivocal. 1 Samuel 15:22-23 states, "**Has the LORD as great delight in burnt offerings and sacrifices, as in obeying the voice of the LORD? Behold, to obey is better than sacrifices, and to heed than the fat of rams, for rebellion is as the sin of witchcraft, and stubbornness is as iniquity and idolatry. Because you have rejected the word of the LORD, he also had rejected you from being king.**"

Saul's faulty foundation led him down a path that would eventually lose him the kingdom. Although he was humble and modest to start with, the power that came with his position eventually revealed a man who was selfish, self-willed and quick to rely on his faulty reasoning rather than on the word of the Most High God. Many of his decisions were aimed at pleasing the people of Israel, (themselves flawed with faulty foundations), rather than on pleasing the Most High God who had placed him in that position of authority as his envoy.

Saul continue to reign as king of Israel for many years after Samuel's pronouncement but he no longer did so with the blessing and guidance of the Lord who had already directed Samuel to anoint David as the new king. For the rest of Saul's reign, he became increasingly paranoid and erratic in his behaviour. After Samuel anointed David, we are told in 1 Samuel 16:14 **"But the spirit of the LORD departed from Saul, and a distressing spirit from the LORD troubled him."** The Lord withdrew from Saul the spirit that he had given him to enable him carry out his royal duties and all the characteristics that had made Saul such an impressive king in his early days on the throne left him. God rejected Saul just as Saul had earlier rejected him and with this rejection, Satan took over Saul's mind to torment and trouble him.

In the last days of Saul's life, his descent into pure evil culminated with him turning to a witch for guidance. How far he had fallen from his lofty heights Saul who had been handpicked by the Lord to do his will, who had been given a new heart and endowed with qualities fit for an emissary of the Lord, who had been personally directed by the prophet of God and assisted by Jehovah himself in the execution of his duties had become a liar, a cheat, a thief and a murderer and finally had turned to agents of Satan for direction.

Saul's lack of obedience to the Most High God, his willfulness, pride and his concern for the approval of people rather than God's approval all stemmed from his faulty foundation. He was unable to love God and rely on him total as he should have, choosing instead of relying on his reasoning, strength and ability to do the work that God had called him to. The result was that he forgot God and ascribed the victories that he had gained to his strength and abilities, thereby losing his kingdom.

As I stated earlier, your foundation will determine if your life will be a success or a failure. A faulty foundation can only take so much success before it begins to crumble. Ultimately, Saul's foundation could not handle the weight of the blessing the Lord had bestowed upon him and as a result, his end was tragic.

CHAPTER 5

JESUS, A SOLID FOUNDATION

We have established that through our common ancestor Adam who passed sin down to the entire human race, we all suffer from faulty foundations. To illustrate how these faulty foundations prevent us from loving God and following his commands, we looked at the example of the children of Israel and King Saul.

These are just two of the countless cases that we can find in the bible, which show the disastrous result that comes onto man whenever he turns his back on God and follows his willful inclinations. The children of Israel demonstrated once and for all that on their own, human beings are unable to submit to God and to consistently obey his word.

What then is the solution to man's faulty foundations? Man's faulty foundations are a result of our sinful nature which is passed onto us upon our birth. God decided that since our faulty foundations were acquired through birth, our new, solid foundations would also have to come to us the same way. For man to gain a new foundation, he would have to receive the new birth.

Our new birth was to be achieved through God's Son, Jesus Christ, who he sent to earth in human form to pay the price for our sin.

Romans 6:23 states, "**For the wages of sin is death, but he gift of God is eternal life in Christ Jesus our Lord.**"

You may ask yourselves why someone had to pay the price for our sin. Could God not just decide to forgive us and give us all new birth? The truth is that sin is a wrong done to God and the consequences of this sin are spiritual and physical death. Even though God loves us and wants to forgive us, before he can do so, atonement must be made for our sins. The dictionary defines atonement as "Amends or reparation made for an injury or wrong".

In the content of the bible, it has to do with the repair of the relationship between God and man. With his sin, man wronged God and so something had to happen for man to be reconciled to God.

Hebrews, 9:22 tells us that without the shedding of blood there is no remission of sins. In the time before Jesus Christ, the Lord instructed the children of Israel to offer orifices to him at specific times. There was also a special "Day of atonement" during which the priest dressed in a simple white garment and performed three acts; the sacrifice and sprinkling of the blood of a single bullock, the killing of the goat of the sin offering and sprinkling of its blood, and the sending off of the scapegoat. These sacrifices were intended to cleanse the nation of Israel from its sin.

Hebrews 10:1-2 states, "**for the law, having a shadow of the good things to come, and not the very image of the things, can never with these same sacrifices, which they offer continually year by year, make those who approach perfect. For then would they not have ceased to be offered? For the worshipers, once purified, would have had no more consciousness of sins.**"

This passage clearly stated that the atonement sacrifice offered by the children of Israel was only a temporary solution as it had to be repeated every year. If the solution were permanent, there would have been no need to make it an annual event.

The permanent solution came into the form of Jesus Christ, who as is stated, in 2 Corinthians 5:21 "Knew no sin" but became a sin offering for us. The question may be raised that since Jesus Christ came to earth as a man, how was he able to avoid inheriting the sinful nature that is inherent in all men?

The fact is that although Jesus Christ was born of a woman, he was conceived by the Holy Spirit. He received his human nature through the Virgin Mary but his divine nature was obtained from

God through the Holy Spirit. It appears that the sin nature is passed to man through the father and not the mother. Support for this view is found in Roman 5:12, which states, "**Therefore, just as through one man sin entered the world, and death through sin, and thus death spread to all men, because all sinned.**"

It was Eve who first sinned but the bible tells us that sin came into the world through Adam.

Having established that Jesus was without sin, we should also note that while he was here on earth, he surfed the same temptations that we did and yet he did not sin. 1 Peter 2:21-24, "**For to this you were called, because Christ also suffered for us, leaving us an example, that you should follow his steps: who committed no sin, nor was deceit found in his mouth, who, when he was reviled, did not revile in return; when he suffered, he did not threaten, but committed himself to him who judges righteously; who himself bore our sins in His own body on the tree, that we, having died to sins, might live for righteousness - by whose stripes you were healed**".

Jesus Christ came to earth without sin and while he was here on earth, he did not allow sin to defile his body as this would have prevented him from fulfilling his primary mission of saving man from his sin. In Matthew 1:21, the Angel Gabriel said of Jesus "And she will bring forth a son, and you shall call his name Jesus, for he will save his people from their sins." God sent his Son to earth, to take human form and live amongst mankind for the specific purpose of saving us from our sin and reconciling us to God.

2 Corinthians 5:18, "**Now all things are of God, who has reconciled us to himself through Jesus Christ, and has given us the ministry of reconciliation.**"

As Jesus remained without blemish throughout his sojourn here on earth, he became the perfect sacrificial lamb upon which our sins could be placed. John the Baptist described Jesus in John 1:29 as "the lamb of God who takes away the sin of the world." Unlike the sacrifice carried out in the old testament times, however, Jesus' sacrifice was God's permanent solution to the problems of man's sin. John 3:16 states, "For God so loved the world that he gave his only begotten son, that whoever believes in him should not perish but have everlasting life."

The new birth that Jesus Christ came to offer to all mankind is spelt out in John 3:3 which reads, "most assuredly, I say to you unless one is born again, he cannot see the kingdom of God." To become born again, the first thing you must do is submit your life to Jesus. You must recognize that you are a sinner and that you cannot save yourself but need Jesus to reconcile you to God. Romans 10:9 reads, "If you confess with your mouth the Lord Jesus and believe in your heart that God has raised Him from the dead, you will be saved".

Once you submit your life to Christ, two things will happen. The first thing that will happen is that your sins will be wiped always. Jesus paid for your sins on the cross at Calvary so that, as is stated in 2 Corinthians 5:21, "we might become the righteousness of God in him."

This means that despite the sinful nature that you were born with God will accept you and treat you as righteous because of the sacrifice that Jesus Christ made for mankind

The second thing that will happen is the Holy Spirit will come into your life to live within you and unite with your human spirit. You who were once spiritually dead will receive new life in Christ. 2 Corinthians 5:17 "**Therefore if anyone is in Christ, he is a new creation; old things have passed away; behold, all things have become new.**" When the holy spirit comes into your life he will thoroughly cleanse you, remove all the dirt in your life and your heart and enable you to live a new life in Christ. The gap that existed between you and God will be swept away; you will be reconciled to him and will have received the right to call him your Father.

The new birth is explained in Romans 6:2-11, "**How shall we who died to sin live any longer in it? Or do you not know that as many of us as were baptized into Christ Jesus were baptized into his death? Therefore we were buried with him through baptism into death, that just as Christ was raised from the dead by the glory of the Father, even so, we also should walk in newness of life. For if we have been united together in the likeness of his death certainly** we also shall be in the likeness of his resurrection, knowing this, that our old man was crucified with him, that the body of sin might be done away with that we should no longer be slaves of sin. For he who has died has been freed from sin. Now if we died with Christ, we believe that we shall also live with him, knowing that Christ, having been raised from the dead, dies no more. Death no longer has dominion over him. For the death that he died, he died to sin once for all; but the life that He lives He lives to God. Likewise, you also, reckon yourselves to be dead indeed to sin, but alive to God in Christ Jesus our Lord."

The idea of the new birth is that our old corrupt nature is crucified with Jesus Christ on the cross of Calvary and the whole body of our sin is removed so that we are no longer slaves to sin. Our death to sin means a resurrection what Jesus Christ to God and a new life of holiness, a new, solid foundation.

What then is the consequences of our new birth on our sinful nature? The first thing is that our spiritual blindness is lifted and our eyes are open to the kingdom of God. John 3:3 states that unless a man is born again, he cannot see the kingdom of God. The only way to God's kingdom and salvation is through Christ. Once we are made new in Christ, we can see the awesomeness of God and bask in his love, mercy and faithfulness towards us.

Our selfish nature is crucified with Christ and we become focused on him and not on ourselves. In Galatians 2:20 apostle Paul states, "I have been crucified with Christ; it is no longer I who live but Christian lives in me." Apostle Paul was saying that he lived in a state of complete and utter dependence on Jesus Christ and no longer relied on his head knowledge to live.

The lust of the flesh is crucified and we begin to exhibit the fruits of the spirit and not the works of our sinful flesh. Galatians 5:22-24 states, "But the fruit of the spirit is love, joy peace, longsuffering, kindness, goodness, faithfulness, gentleness, self-control. Against such, there is no law. And those who are Christ's have crucified the flesh with its passions and desires."

All who are genuine Christians are no longer subject to the desires or the influence of their flesh as they have nailed their flesh to cross with Jesus. Rather they begin to manifest the fruits of the spirit which are the characteristic that the Holy Spirit produces within them.

Our worldliness is crucified and our focus is removed from the things of the world to the things of God. In Galatians 6:14 Apostle Paul said, "**But God forbid that I should boast except in the cross of our Lord Jesus Christ, by whom the world had been crucified to me, and I to the world.**" Apostle Paul was saying here that the world had lost its power over him and all worldly pursuits and desires no longer had any attraction for him. His love and affection were removed from the things of the world and transferred to the things of God.

We also receive the grace to help us in our weakness. 2 Corinthians 2:19 states, "My grace is sufficient for you, for My strength is made perfect in weakness," Therefore most gladly I will rather boast in my infirmities, that the power of Christ may rest upon me." In of ourselves, all human beings are weak and prone to fall. The key to receiving God's grace to help us in our weakness is to recognize that weakness and throw ourselves upon his strength.

With our corrupt nature crucified with Jesus Christ and our old man dead, our faulty foundations are also laid to rest. Our new births bring with them new solid foundations, resting on our Lord Jesus Christ in whom we are made perfect. These should be the conditions of all who call themselves born again Christians. How then can we explain Christians who still exhibit the signs of faulty foundations? We will examine this in the next chapter.

CHAPTER 6
CHRISTIANS WITH FAULTY FOUNDATONS

Once we become born again children of God, our old faulty foundations are wiped away and we start afresh with new foundations on which we can build successful lives. This is the only way that we can fulfil our divine destiny and become who God created us to be.

Unfortunately, the lives of many so-called born again children of God are still manifesting signs of faulty foundations. The bible tells us in 2 Corinthians 5: 17 "**Therefore if anyone is in Christ, he is a new creation; old things have passed away; behold, all things have become new.**" This means that once you become born again, you have Christ dwelling within your heart and you become a new creature. While in the past you were a child of Satan, you become a child of God; while you were a slave to sin and exhibited the works of the flesh, you are freed from sin and begin to exhibit the fruits of the spirit; while in the past your focus was on the things of this world and accumulating as much of them as possible, you now begin to store up for yourself treasures in heaven. In short, you gain a new life with a new mind, a new focus and a new inspiration from the almighty God.

If you profess to be a born again Christian yet you are still the same person you were before you gave your life to Christ then something is wrong. The bible does not tell a lie and genuine Christians do become transformed by their new birth. If you have not become a new person then you need to examine yourself and your relationship with God very closely.

One of the most obvious signs of a faulty foundation in someone who calls himself a Christian is a bad character. In chapter four, we looked at the example of King Saul and how his bad character cost him his kingdom. So many Christians today show signs of similar character and some of them even openly admit to having such bad traits. This is something to be ashamed of because as a true Christians, you can't have a bad character. You find professing Christians who are rude, insolent and cannot show respect to whom it is due. They are quick to take offence, quick to get angry and throw tantrums and quick to throw insults and fight others.

Nowadays, it is common for someone to leave the church and immediately end up fighting on a bus or in the street.

One lesson that I learned recently is that spirituality without good character makes Christianity unattractive. We should put this on the doors of our homes to remind ourselves. You may have read the whole Bible many times over. You may be able to quote scriptures, speak in tongues and pray powerful prayers, but if your character is awful, if you are quick to get angry and shout at others if you always seem to be spoiling for a fight, then you cannot call yourself a child of God. If you exhibit bad character traits when you go out to evangelize nobody would want to embrace your religion because of your behaviour.

How many of us have put people off and driven people out of church because of our characters? Our lives are supposed to minister to others and lead them to Christ.

Other so-called children of God are filled with pride, God has not even blessed them yet but they are extremely pompous and proud and hate to take correction from anyone. They are quick to justify their sin and find it hard to repent when they have done wrong. If God were to bless them more than he had now, who on this earth would be able to speak to them and tell them the truth about their behaviour?

Taking Saul as an example we saw how he always attempted to justify his disobedience to God, giving excuses that were meaningless in the sight of God.

God does not care what other people around you think, he cares that you are following the instructions that he gave you. If he sends his prophet to correct you and to warn you about your behaviour and you reject the words of the prophet then you are rejecting God and running the risk that God will proclaim his judgment on you just as he did on Saul.

1 Samuel 2:30 states, "**for those who honour Me I will honour, and those who despise me shall be lightly esteemed.**"

So many Christians Nowadays do not give honour to God and his anointed. What does it mean to give honour to God? is id doing things that will please God. Before God prospered you, there were certain things that you said that you would always do for him. Are you still doing those things? Before you became big, you used to be punctual in church, you used to crawl on the floor and worship God fervently; can you still do these things? If the blessings that God has placed on you have caused you to turn away from him, then you are not giving honour to God, you are not acknowledging that it is he who was responsible for the heights you have risen to.

Other so-called Christians look down on those who are not as wealthy as they are. They refuse to associate with them because they feel that their wealth somehow makes them better than anyone else. They believe that their status in society makes them special and gives them privileges that do not apply to others. They forget the times of their small beginning and are filled with pride. If you are truly a child of God with a new foundation, pride will be far from you. There will be no issue of which class you belong to as you will see everyone as a child of God and you will respect them equally. You will respect those who are older than you and you will give the same respect to those who are rich as you give to those who are not. When God blesses you, your attitude will not change and people will not be able to tell from your behaviour that there is a difference in you.

We saw when we looked at the reign of King Saul that at the end God was sorry that he had ever made Saul king. In 1 Samuel 15:11, God said to Samuel, "I greatly regret that I have set up Saul as king, for he has turned back from following me, and has not performed my commandments." It is possible for God to be sorry that he ever blessed someone or raised them to certain heights. If right now you are asking God to bless you and you do not deal with the issue of your bad character, when God does bless you and you reach the heights that you have longed for, Satan will use that bad character to bring you down.

Many so-called children of God are consumed by worldliness. They want to be worthy of being called a child of God, a prophet, an evangelist and so on but they have not yet killed their flesh and died to the world. They allow themselves to be occupied by the things of the world and to be swayed by what the world thinks of them.

A few years ago, I ministered about the issue of earrings, I told my congregation that in the past, earrings were only worn by slaves to indicate who their master was and that as children of God, women should not be wearing earnings. After the sermon, I noticed that some of the women in church stopped wearing earrings and I was encouraged because I felt that the word of God had ministered to them. Gradually, however, they began to were their earrings again. They had gone out into the world without earrings and because the world is not used to seeing women without earrings, they regarded them as strange. To blend with the world and not stand out from the crowd, these women want back to wearing their earrings. They were not able to stand the pressure and quickly succumbed to the demands and expectations of the world.

Putting the issues of earnings aside, when the world looks at you, can they identify you as a Christian? True children of God with new foundations are supposed to be correct representatives of Christ here on earth. They should embody all that Christ was about while he was here, both in their behaviour and their appearance. People should look at you and be able to see that there is something different about you from the way you dress and comport yourself. You should not be wearing the latest body revealing styles just because it is in fashion.

If you are truly born again, the things that the world responds to will not interest you and the ways of the world will be irritating to you. Worldly entertainments like parties, drinking, smoking and dancing will no longer feature in your life. You would prefer to listen to inspirational music and not the music of the world. However, this is not the case with many children of God nowadays. They know all the latest songs in town and can dance the newest dances steps better than those in the secular world.

When it comes to the opportunity of being seen as a child of God or making money which would you choose? We say that everything about this country is corrupt but if you happen to find yourself in a powerful position in the government would you show that you are different, that you are a child of God and do your job honestly or would you be like everyone else and enrich yourself too? So many so-called children of God enter into government and bring the name of the Lord into disrepute. They profess God with their mouths but in their actions, they are just as bad as all the others. That is why in this country we have so many Christians but such a high level of corruption. The heavens are taking a record of everyone's actions every day to determine if they are truly who they confess to being or whether they are just hypocrites.

In his time here on earth, Jesus spoke often about hypocrisy. More than once, He accused the Pharisees of hypocrisy because they were quick to judge others while they were doing wrong. If the world can look at you and call you a hypocrite, that is a disgrace to the almighty. It is easier for people to be Christians in church than to be Christians at home or in their places of work. If you act holier than thou in church but at home, you can shout at your husband or your house girl, then you are being a hypocrite.

Once you become a born again child of God with new foundations, then your life is supposed to go a certain way. Your new solid foundations should allow God to build new blessings and new prosperities onto your life. If however, you are experiencing the following issues, then you need to re-examine your life to determine why your faulty foundations are still militating against you.

1. You are a regular participant in deliverance programmes.

Deliverance never seems to last in your life, no sooner have you completed one deliverance programmed than you have to undergo another one.

2. You have remained in one position for a long time with no appreciable change.

3. You find it difficult to stand on your own and are always looking to others for approval or affirmation.

4. You often experience mysterious problems that you cannot explain and that are beyond your understanding.

5. Your life is a constant struggle and you experience one problem after another. You solve one problem only for another one to suddenly appear.

6. You always experience failure at the edge of success. Just when you think that you are about to achieve a breakthrough, something prevents it from coming to pass.

7. Your sleep is a battleground and you are always fighting demons or masquerades in your dreams.

8. You are surrounded by cobwebs everywhere you go.

9. People hate you without good reason and you cannot find favour anywhere you go.

10. You suffer from an illness that has been in your family for generations and for which there seems to be no medical cure.

If any of these things are present in our life as a child of God, then your foundations are still faulty and you must fix them once and for all if you want to live a successful life.

CHAPTER 7

THE ONLY SOLUTION

Why is it that born again children of God still have faulty foundations? Why have their lives and their situations remained the same, although they have given their lives to Jesus and are practising Christians?

In Philippians 2:12-13, apostle Paul enjoins the converted people of Philippi to "work out your salvation with fear and trembling: for it is God who works in you both to will and to do for his good pleasure."

As children of God, we need to work out our salvation to ensure that it endures and that the prize of eternal life will be ours at the end of the day. We are told in 2 Peter 1:10 to be diligent to make your call and election sure".

This does not mean that our good works will earn us a ticket to heaven, nor does it mean that we can do anything in ourselves to atone for our past wrongs. This is impossible and in any case, Jesus has already given his life to atone for our sins.

What the bible passage does mean is that we have a personal responsibility to repent and turn away from our sins. We are to believe in our saviour Jesus Christ and work together with the Holy Spirit to resist all the temptations of the world which may take us away from God's presence.

Hebrews 12:1 states, **"Therefore we also, since we are surrounded by so great a loud of witness, let us lay aside every weight, and the sin which so easily ensnares us, and let us run with endurance the race that is set before us."** We should note that we can't endure till the end on our own because as the passage states, it is very easy to be trapped by the enemy and to be "moved away from the hope of the gospel" (Colossians 1:23).

This is why it is important to throw ourselves completely at the mercy of the Holy Spirit and ask him to take control of our lives. The Holy Spirit is a gentleman and will not impose his wishes upon us; we have to choose to change.

We are told in Philippians 2:13 that God is ready to work in us to achieve our goal and in fact, all that we do depends on God working in us. You will recall our sinful nature itself is weak and without the grace of God, our bid to remain steadfast would surely fall before we have even begun. It is the grace of God working within us through the holy spirit that enables us to want to do the right thing and empowers us to do it. Galatians 5:16, "**I say then: walk in the spirit, and you shall not fulfil the lust of the flesh**". Only when we are walking in total unison with God will we be able to hold on to our salvation.

In chapter one we established that the foundation is the most important part of the building as the quality of the foundation will determine whether the building will remain standing or if it will eventually collapse. We compared the foundation of a life to the foundation of a building and we stated that the success or failure of your life is completely dependent on the nature of your foundation. We also clarified that your foundation is made up of the beliefs you subscribe to, which will eventually determine your thoughts, your words and your actions.

The only foundation that a true born again child of God should have is Jesus Christ. He is the only solid foundation. As Isaiah 28:16 states, "**Therefore thus says the Lord God: "Behold, I lay in Zion a stone for a foundation, a tried stone, a precious cornerstone, a sure foundation; whoever believes will not at hastily.**"

Whoever builds his foundation on Jesus Christ will never be defeated by the storms that life may bring; he will never be shaken or uprooted. A man who looks to Jesus Christ for wisdom and validation, who holds on to him for protection and security and who turns to him for happiness and reassurance will have cause to rejoice at the end of the day. A man who professes to be a

Christian but who gains his sense of significance, security and self-worth from anything other than Christ is only deceiving himself and at the end of the day, he will be swept away by the storms of life and cast out with the rest of the unbelievers.

Jesus had something to say about this in Matthew 7: 24-27 when he contrasted the man who built his house on the sand with the man who but his house pond the rock. He said,

"Not everyone who says to me, 'Lord, Lord', shall enter the kingdom of heaven, but he who does the will of my father in heaven. Many will say to me in that day, 'Lord, Lord, have we not prophesied in our name, cast out demons in your name, and done many wonders in your name?' And then I will declare to them, 'I never knew you; depart from Me, you who practice lawlessness!' "Therefore whoever hears these sayings of mine, and does them, I will liken him to a wise man who built his house on the rock: and the rain descended, the floods came and the wind blew and beat on that house; and it did not fall for it was founded on the rock. But everyone who hears these sayings of mine, and does not do them, will be like a foolish man who built his house on the sand "and the rain descended, the floods came, and the winds blew and beat on that house; and it fell. And great was its fall."

With this parable, Jesus was showing us that the only way that we can guarantee our salvation is not just by listening to his words and professing with our mouths that we are his children but by actually living according to his teaching. Many would number themselves amongst Jesus Christ but in this bible passage, he warns them that they will be rejected when the time for judgment arrives. They are deceiving themselves and mocking Christ if they believe that just by the public assertion that they are born again children of God they automatically qualify for all the benefits that come with it.

The truth is that the majority of so-called Christians are focused on this world and on what they can achieve here, rather than on building up treasures for themselves in heaven.

In Matthew 6:19-21 Jesus enjoins us, **"Do not lay up for yourselves treasures on earth where moth and rust destroy and where thieves break in and steal; but lay up for yourselves**

treasures in heaven, where neither moth nor rust destroys and where thieves do not break in and steal. For where your treasure is, there your heart will be also."

When we are building our lives here on earth, our main focus should be on building them in such a way that we will gain eternal life in heaven. This thought is very far from the mind of most of the people who called themselves born again Christians.

In Matthew 6:33 Jesus advises us as follows: "**But seek first the kingdom of God and his righteousness, and all these things shall be added to you.**" When we allow the quest for worldly goods to consume us, we remove our focus from the Most High God, who is ready to be our provider and our only source of all that we need.

Philippians 4:19 "**And my God shall supply all your need according to his riches in glory by Christ Jesus.**"

The way to attain your solid foundation is to fall on the cornerstone that is Jesus Christ and become broken so that you will be recreated in his image. Only these who are broken, and who allow themselves to be rebuilt on the solid rock can claim to be his children. Only those who have truly made him their anchor and who follow his commands at all times, no matter how difficult it may be can expect to obtain new, solid and lasting foundations. Doing this requires diligence and commitment. Your focus must be completely removed from the world and be fixed on your heavenly destination.

Many people claim to be heaven-bound but when you examine their lives you will see that rather than building on the rock that is Jesus Christ, they have built their lives upon the sand. They have bought into the fallacy that is "modern Christianity" and even though they are called Christians and may be workers in the house of God, even though they may fast and pray and appear to be committed to the things of God, they are far from being what the Lord expects his children to be.

At the end of the day, every man's work will be tried to see the kind of foundation that he has built his life upon 1 Corinthians 3:11-14 states, "**For no other foundation can anyone lay than that which is laid, which is Jesus Christ. Now if anyone builds on this foundation with gold, silver, precious stone, wood, hay, straw,**

each one's work will become clear; for the day will declare it, because it will be revealed by fire, and the fire will test each one's work, of what sort it is. If anyone's work which he has built on it endures, he will receive a reward."

Everyone's work will be tested by fire and those who are built upon the solid rock will earn the right to be called heaven's stars, stars like Shadrach, Meshach and Abednego and went through pain, shame and persecution but would not waver in their devotion to God; who disdained worldly pursuits and criticism and kept their focus on their heavenly goals who drew their strength and hope from the Most High God, trusting that no matter what it looked like, ultimately, he would not fail them.

In conclusion, Jesus Christ is the only foundation on which you should build your life. If you want to withstand the storms of life and emerge victorious at the end of the race, you must turn to him, surrender yourself to Him and commit to diligently following his leading and his word in all circumstances. Your foundation in Christ will not be established merely by your confession; your attitude and your works will determine if you truly are building your life upon the solid rock of Jesus.

Ultimately, he is the only one who will enable you to stand firm through the trials and tribulations that you will face in this life. If you build your life on anything else, eventually it will fail you. Recall the chorus to that popular hymn "The Solid Rock".

"On Christ the solid rock I stand
All other ground is sinking sand
All other ground is sinking sand.
Anything but Jesus is sinking sand; build your life on him alone.

Prayer points:

1. O Lord save me from myself, in the name of Jesus.

2. O Lord, let me be lost in you in the name of Jesus.

3. O Lord, let self die in me and let Christ live instead, in the name of Jesus.

Pastor Seyi Ogunorunyinka, a minister of the Gospel, is anointed and gifted in healing and deliverance, spiritual warfare and in the power of the Holy Spirit. A prophet called by GOD and being used to release empowerment for abundance and victory in the lives of believers. Through his ministry, lives are being touched daily with the power of the Holy Spirit leading to peace and restoration to GOD's abundant life.

Pastor Seyi Ogunorunyinka is the Pastor of the Promised Land Restoration Ministries (PLRM) based in Lagos, Nigeria. PLRM is a ministry standing on the truth of GOD'S word and whose vision is propelled by the Holiness and Righteousness of GOD.